Awesome
African
Animals!

Elephants Are Awesome!

by Martha E. H. Rustad

Consultant: Jackie Gai, DVM
Captive Wildlife Veterinarian

CAPSTONE PRESS
a capstone imprint

A+ Books are published by Capstone Press,
1710 Roe Crest Drive, North Mankato, Minnesota 56003
www.capstonepub.com

Library of Congress Cataloging-in-Publication Data
Rustad, Martha E. H. (Martha Elizabeth Hillman), 1975- author.
 Elephants are awesome! / by Martha E. H. Rustad.
    pages cm. — (A+ books. Awesome African animals)
 Summary: "Describes the characteristics, habitat, behavior, life cycle, and threats to elephants living in the wild
of Africa"—Provided by publisher.
 Audience: Ages 5–8.
 Audience: K to grade 3.
 Includes bibliographical references and index.
 ISBN 978-1-4914-1760-7 (library binding)
 ISBN 978-1-4914-1766-9 (paperback)
 ISBN 978-1-4914-1772-0 (eBook PDF)
1. Elephants—Juvenile literature. 2. Animals—Africa—Juvenile literature. I. Title.

 QL737.P98R87 2015
 599.67—dc23   2014023669

For Mac, Marit, and Nash. —MEHR

Editorial Credits
Mari Bolte and Erika Shores, editors; Cynthia Della-Rovere, designer; Svetlana Zhurkin, media researcher;
Morgan Walters, production specialist

Photo Credits
iStockphotos: Serge_Vero, 24—25; Newscom: Ingram Publishing, 27 (bottom); Shutterstock: Alexander
Kuguchin, 4 (bottom), Amy Nichole Harris, 5, Andre Klopper, 22 (top), BGSmith, cover (top), Black Sheep Media
(grass), back cover and throughout, Chris Erasmus, 22 (bottom), Costas Anton Dumitrescu, 20—21, Donovan
van Staden, 9, Eric Isselee, back cover, 13, 15 (top), 32, Four Oaks, 10 (left), 12, 23, Gerrit_de_Vries, 18 (bottom),
Hector Conesa, cover (bottom), Jez Bennett, 10—11, Konstantin Goldenberg, 14, Marie-Anne Aberson, 19, Mark
Bridger, 15 (bottom), Matej Hudovernik, 26, moizhusein, 6—7, Nobby Clarke, 21 (top), NREY, 24 (top), Peter
Betts, 27 (top), Photo Love, cover (middle), 1, 11 (right), PlusONE, 4 (top), Richard Peterson, 8, Steffen Foerster,
28—29, Tobie Oosthuizen, 16, Villiers Steyn, 17, 18 (top)

Note to Parents, Teachers, and Librarians
This Awesome African Animals book uses full color photographs and a nonfiction format to introduce
the concept of elephants. *Elephants Are Awesome!* is designed to be read aloud to a pre-reader or to be
read independently by an early reader. Photographs help listeners and early readers understand the
text and concepts discussed. The book encourages further learning by including the following sections:
Table of Contents, Glossary, Read More, Internet Sites, and Index. Early readers may need assistance
using these features.

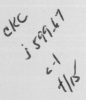

Printed in China by Nordica.
0914/CA21401520
092014   008470NORDS15

Table of Contents

Elephants at Home

Rumble, rumble! The savanna ground shakes. A herd of African elephants thunders by.

These elephants make their homes in many African habitats. They travel from savannas to forests to mountains. They ramble from deserts to swamps.

Just keep walking! Elephants migrate across Africa. Strong, solid legs carry their heavy gray bodies. They look for food and water.

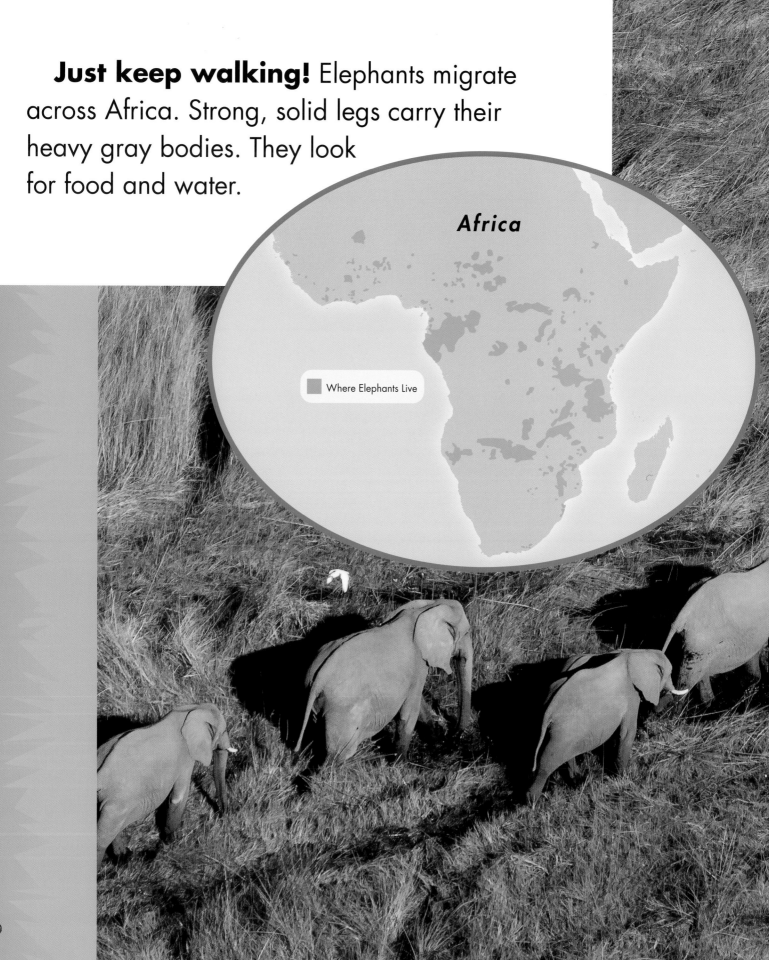

Africa

Where Elephants Live

Elephants travel hundreds of miles each year. They walk about 5 miles (8 kilometers) per hour. In short bursts elephants can reach speeds of 25 miles (40 km) per hour.

African elephants are the biggest animals on land. They are larger than Asian elephants. All its life an elephant never stops growing. They weigh as much as 8 tons (7 metric tons). That is almost as much as a school bus.

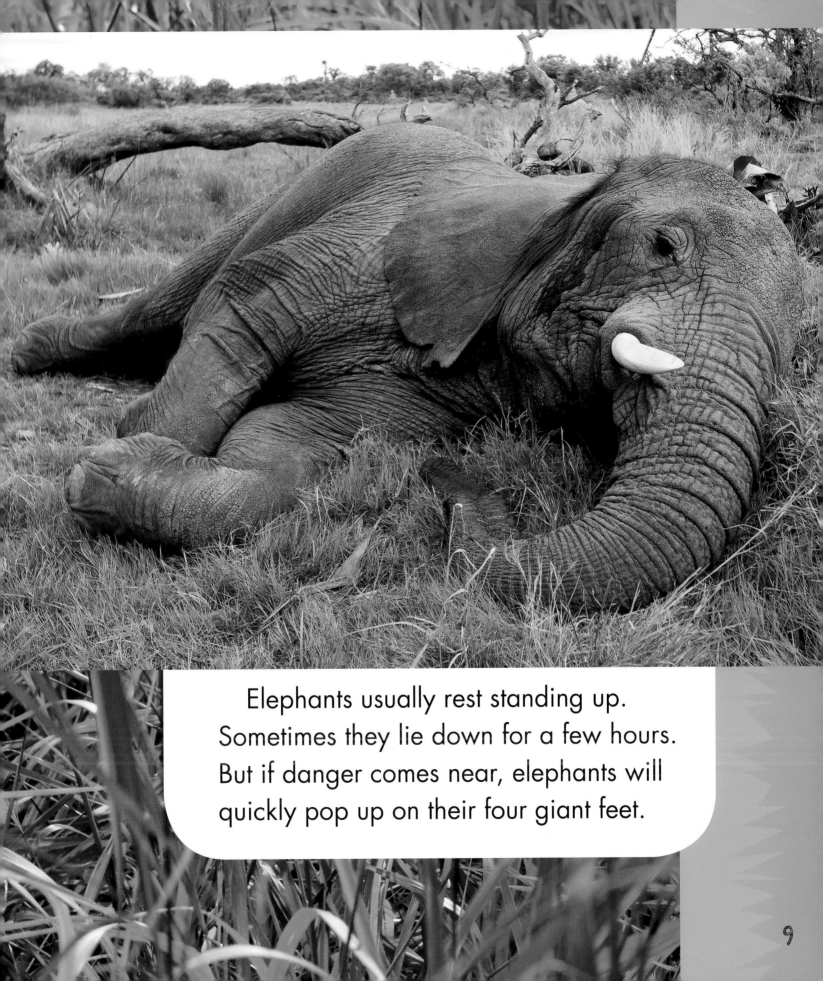

Elephants usually rest standing up. Sometimes they lie down for a few hours. But if danger comes near, elephants will quickly pop up on their four giant feet.

From Trunk to Tail

Sniff! Elephants lift their trunks to smell. They also breathe through this long nose.

Two tips on the end of a trunk work like fingers. Elephants use their trunks to grab leaves from branches. Their strong trunks pull trees from the ground.

Dig! Tusks are helpful tools. Elephants use tusks to dig holes to find water. Tusks help them peel bark from trees. Tusks are also used for fighting.

Elephants use their ears to do more than listen. Large ears help elephants stay cool. Blood flows through their thin ears. Elephants flap their ears to cool the blood. **Thwap!**

Grab my tail! There is a tuft of hair at the end of an elephant's tail. A very young elephant calf may hold an adult's tail with its trunk.

Hungry, Thirsty, and Hot

Chomp, chomp! Enormous elephants eat and eat. They spend all day eating to fuel their big bodies. An adult male elephant eats up to 400 pounds (180 kilograms) of food each day.

Elephants munch plants and grasses. They gobble fruit and seeds. Four wide, flat molars chew and chew.

Slurp! Hot, thirsty elephants drink water.
Adults drink up to 50 gallons (190 liters) every day.

Squirt! Elephant
trunks suck up water
like a straw. Then the
elephants shoot water
into their mouths.

Spray! Elephants spray water on their bodies to cool off. They sprinkle dirt and mud on their wrinkled skin. It works like sunscreen.

Elephant Families

Follow me! The oldest female in the family is called a matriarch. She leads her sisters, her daughters, and their calves. The matriarch remembers where to find food and water for her family.

Groups of families are called herds. Herds gather at watering holes. Elephants touch and twist trunks to say hello.

Squeak! A hungry calf drinks milk from its mother. Calves look like small adults. The entire family cares for calves. They teach them, play with them, and keep them safe.

Male elephants leave their family around age 10. Groups of young males sometimes live together. But many male elephants live alone. Females stay with their family for life. Elephants live up to 70 years.

Staying Safe

Trumpet! Elephants warn each other of danger. Only a few predators try to attack elephants. But elephants watch out for lions, crocodiles, and hyenas. An elephant family forms a circle. They keep young and sick elephants safe.

People are the biggest danger to elephants. People build homes in the paths where elephants travel. Elephants have fewer safe places to live. Some hunters kill elephants for their ivory tusks.

Look! Snap a picture! Tourists visit reserves to see elephants. A reserve is a safe place for elephants. People can help elephants by saving the habitat of these awesome African animals.

Glossary

calf (kaf)—a young elephant

ivory (EYE-vur-ee)—the hard, creamy-white material of an animal's tusk

matriarch (MAY-tree-ARK)—the female leader of a group or herd

migrate (MYE-grate)—to move from one place to another when seasons change or to look for food

molar (MOH-lur)—a wide tooth used to chew food

predator (PRED-uh-tur)—an animal that hunts other animals for food

reserve (ri-ZURV)—an area of land set aside by the government for a special purpose, such as protecting plants and animals

savanna (suh-VAN-uh)—a flat, grassy area of land with few or no trees

tourist (TOOR-ist)—a person who travels and visits places for fun or adventure

trunk (TRUNK)—the elephant's long nose and upper lip

tusk (TUHSK)—a very long, pointed tooth that sticks out when the mouth is closed

Read More

Murray, Julie. *Elephants*. African Animals. Minneapolis: ABDO Pub. Co., 2012.

O'Connell, Caitlin. *A Baby Elephant in the Wild*. New York: Houghton Mifflin Harcourt Publishing Company, 2014.

Perepeczko, Jenny. *Moses: The True Story of an Elephant Baby*. New York: Atheneum Books for Young Readers, 2014.

Internet Sites

FactHound offers a safe, fun way to find Internet sites related to this book. All of the sites on FactHound have been researched by our staff.

Here's all you do:
Visit *www.facthound.com*
Type in this code: 9781491417607

 **Super-cool stuff!** Check out projects, games and lots more at **www.capstonekids.com**

Critical Thinking Using the Common Core

1. Look at the picture on pages 24–25. Describe what you see in the picture. Then read the text. (Integration of Knowledge and Ideas)

2. Why do elephants travel so far to find food and water? (Key Ideas and Details)

3. Describe the dangers an elephant faces every day. (Key Ideas and Details)

Index

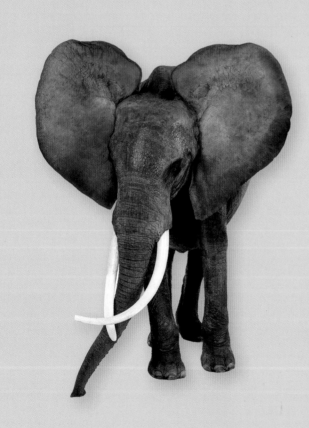